THE
KNOTS
HANDBOOK

Barry Mault
Illustrated by Gillian Blease

WARNING

Children should always be supervised when learning to tie knots. Never allow a child to place a cord or rope around a part of the body, their own or anyone else's. You are strongly advised to seek professional instruction before using knots in a potentially hazardous or dangerous situation.

While all reasonable care has been taken to ensure the accuracy of the information, the publisher can take no responsibility for the use of the methods described.

This edition published in 2024 by Arcturus Publishing Limited
26/27 Bickels Yard, 151-153 Bermondsey Street,
London SE1 3HA

Authors: Barry Mault and William Potter
Additional text: William Potter
Illustrator: Gillian Blease
Cover illustrator: Rhys Jefferys
Design: Duck Egg Blue
Editors: Donna Gregory and Becca Clunes

CH007352NT
Supplier 29, Date 1122, PI 00003057

Printed in China

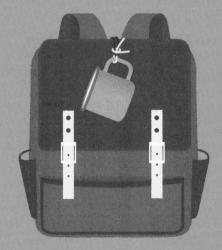

Contents

Introducing Knots

The oldest known length of rope is from Egypt. It is believed to be 4,000 years old and was probably used on a ship. But there is archeological evidence that people were using simple ropes long before this. As a rope isn't much use without a knot, knots must have been around for a very long time too.

While other fastenings have been invented in the last 4,000 years, sometimes there's nothing better than an old-fashioned knot. These knots aren't invented, but discovered or rediscovered after years of not being used. As anyone who has tried to unravel a tangle of string knows, knots can appear like magic!

Until the last century, ropes were usually made from cotton, hemp, and other plants, but these days rope is generally manufactured from synthetic material, such as nylon. These materials are often more slippery, which means that some old sailors' knots are not as reliable as they once were. Different knots may need to be used, so knowing more than one knot for the same task is useful.

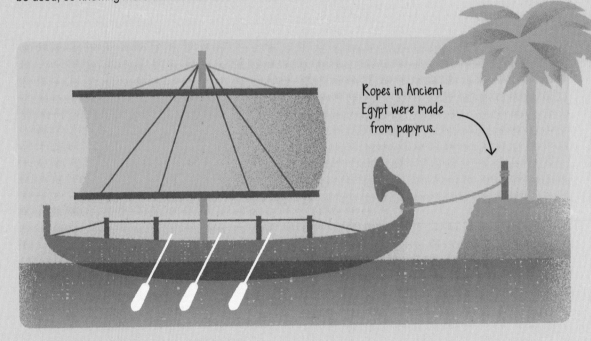

Ropes in Ancient Egypt were made from papyrus.

Knot Names
Names can be very confusing in the world of knots—some knots have a few different names. In this book, the names have been chosen to match each knot's current use.

Knot Terminology

Here are some basic explanations to help get you started:

Standing part The end of a rope (or cord) that isn't used to create a knot. This is also referred to as the **hanging part** when a rope is suspended from another object.

Working end The end of a rope used to create a knot.

Bight A curve in a rope. If the curve is completely closed it becomes a loop.

Loop A circle in a rope, the ends of which are either joined or cross over one another.

A more comprehensive glossary can be found on page 95.

Knots in Use: Strength and Security

When choosing a knot you need to consider two things—strength and security.

Knot Strength

Rope or cord made from natural materials can weaken when a knot is tied in it. Modern synthetic rope, however, has a higher initial strength, so it is less prone to wear and tear.

Knots are stronger when the load (the amount of weight the rope has to carry or support) is applied gradually. If the load is applied suddenly, e.g. by attaching a heavy weight and dropping it from a great height, then the rope or cord may break.

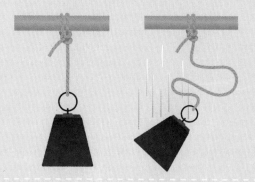

Knot Security

All knots depend on friction. Friction is a force that slows down the movement of two objects sliding, or trying to slide, against each other.

Knot security is based on how likely—or unlikely—the ropes or cords are to slip against each other when they are tied in a knot. It is usually far more important than knot strength. Most knots tend to slip a little at first, as the knot tightens and before friction takes over. Certain materials and knots slip more easily than others—for example, any ordinary knot tied in fishing line is unlikely to hold as the material is so slippery.

One of the most important factors in knot security is making sure the knot is properly tightened. Always take a few moments to check it—the more complex the knot, the more important this is.

CHAPTER 1: BASIC KNOTS & BENDS

In this first chapter there are some simple knots to learn, plus several bends.
Bends are knots that join two or more ropes together to make one longer rope.
If the ropes are made of different material or are different thicknesses they are more
likely to slip undone, so you need to take extra care to make sure they are secure.

When choosing a knot, think about whether you will need to untie the ropes again. The
zeppelin bend can be untied easily but the fisherman's knot is almost impossible to undo!

Overhand Knot

Try this simple knot to get you started. You probably already know how to do it.

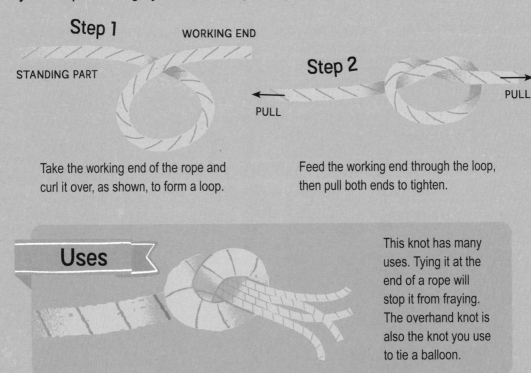

Step 1

WORKING END

STANDING PART

Step 2

PULL

PULL

Take the working end of the rope and
curl it over, as shown, to form a loop.

Feed the working end through the loop,
then pull both ends to tighten.

Uses

This knot has many
uses. Tying it at the
end of a rope will
stop it from fraying.
The overhand knot is
also the knot you use
to tie a balloon.

Figure 8 Knot

If the overhand knot is too small for the job, try this slightly thicker knot instead.

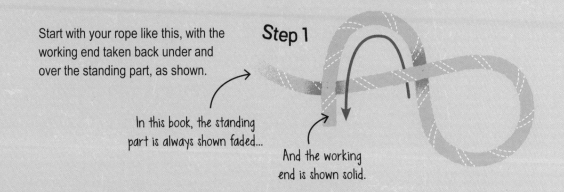

Start with your rope like this, with the working end taken back under and over the standing part, as shown.

Step 1

In this book, the standing part is always shown faded...

And the working end is shown solid.

Step 2

PULL

PULL

Take the working end under and back through the original loop, then pull both ends tight.

Uses

This is a good stopper knot for a rope handle on a bucket, or on a swing seat.

Ashley's Stopper Knot

This knot was invented by Clifford Ashley, an American sailor and knot expert, who was inspired by the ropes he saw on the local oyster fishing boats. This tight, thick knot is ideal for stopping a rope or cord passing through a hole.

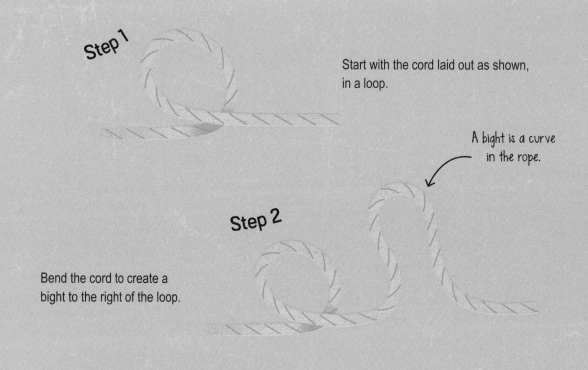

Step 1

Start with the cord laid out as shown, in a loop.

A bight is a curve in the rope.

Step 2

Bend the cord to create a bight to the right of the loop.

Step 3

PULL

Pull the bight through the loop as shown. This creates a slip knot. Tighten the knot around the neck of this loop by pulling on the standing part.

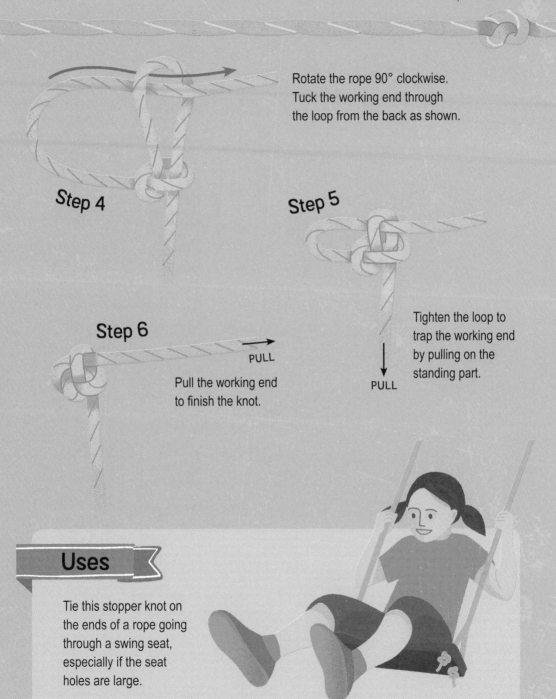

Rotate the rope 90° clockwise. Tuck the working end through the loop from the back as shown.

Step 4

Step 5

Tighten the loop to trap the working end by pulling on the standing part.

PULL

Step 6

PULL

Pull the working end to finish the knot.

Uses

Tie this stopper knot on the ends of a rope going through a swing seat, especially if the seat holes are large.

Albright Knot

This is a simple angling knot used to attach fine nylon thread to thicker cord. It is also useful for attaching cord to thick wire to make the wire easier to pull.

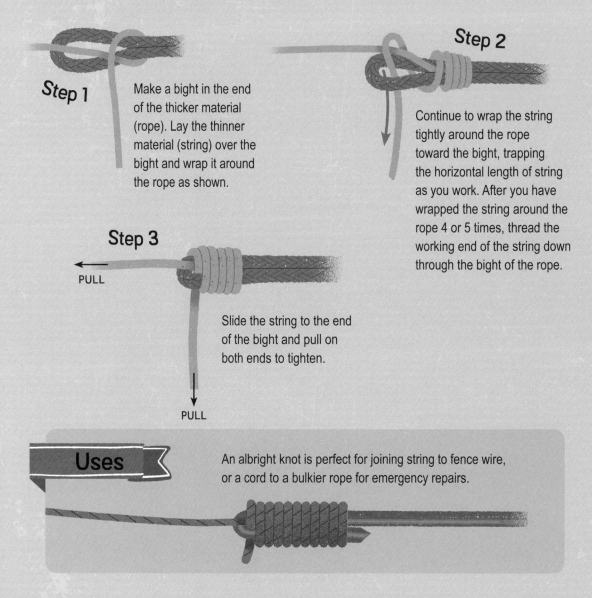

Step 1

Make a bight in the end of the thicker material (rope). Lay the thinner material (string) over the bight and wrap it around the rope as shown.

Step 2

Continue to wrap the string tightly around the rope toward the bight, trapping the horizontal length of string as you work. After you have wrapped the string around the rope 4 or 5 times, thread the working end of the string down through the bight of the rope.

Step 3

PULL

Slide the string to the end of the bight and pull on both ends to tighten.

PULL

Uses

An albright knot is perfect for joining string to fence wire, or a cord to a bulkier rope for emergency repairs.

Carrick Bend

Used aboard ships to join big, heavy towing or mooring ropes, this is a very secure knot for joining two ropes or cords. Even under load it can still be worked loose and untied. Method 1 can be a little bit tricky to remember, but method 2 is easier.

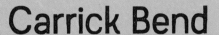

Method 1

Make sure the working ends and standing parts are in the right place.

Step 1

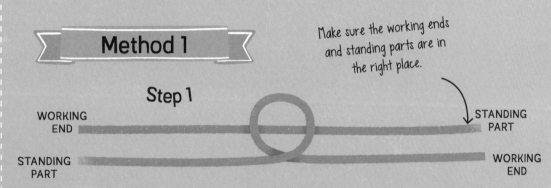

WORKING END

STANDING PART

STANDING PART

WORKING END

Lay the first rope (shown here in blue) horizontally, then create a loop as shown above. Lay the second rope (shown in orange) underneath the loop of the first rope, with the working end to the left.

Step 2

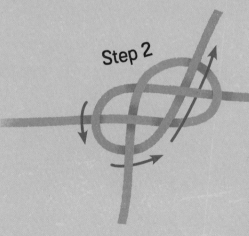

Reposition the working end of the first rope so it is pointing downward. Now take the working end of the second rope down and over the standing part of the first rope. Continue to thread the second rope in an under-over-under-over sequence, as shown. The second rope finishes with the working end on top of the loop of the first rope.

Tighten the knot by pulling on both working ends. Your finished knot should look like this.

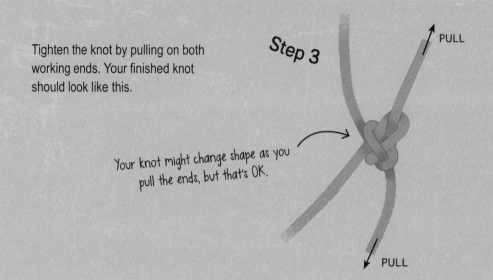

Step 3

PULL

Your knot might change shape as you pull the ends, but that's OK.

PULL

Uses

Tied using either method, the carrick bend is a strong knot. It's useful for joining ropes of similar thickness together—perfect for a tug of war match!

Pull as hard as you like. The knot won't slip!

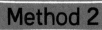
Method 2

Step 1

Make a bight in each rope with the working ends on the outside.

Step 2

Place one bight over the other at an angle, as shown.

Step 3

Take the working end of the top bight and lead it under the bottom rope, then up through its own bight. Repeat for the working end of the bottom bight, but this time go up and over the top rope, then down through its own bight. Adjust the knot if you need to, so the ends don't slip out, then pull steadily on all ends to tighten the knot.

Fisherman's Knot

The fisherman's knot is an excellent, reliable knot originally used by anglers to attach a fishing line to a hook—hence the name. Often used by climbers, it won't slip and is very strong.

Once pulled together and tightened it is almost impossible to undo, making it a great knot for ropes that need to be permanently joined.

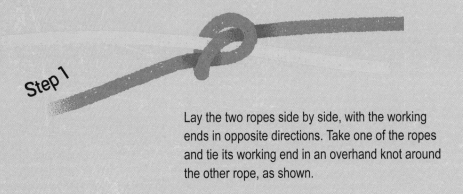

Step 1

Lay the two ropes side by side, with the working ends in opposite directions. Take one of the ropes and tie its working end in an overhand knot around the other rope, as shown.

This knot is simply created from two overhand knots.

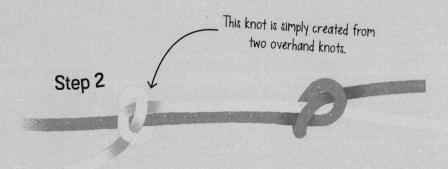

Step 2

Repeat Step 1 with the length of rope that doesn't already have a knot in it, by tying its working end around the standing part of the other rope.

Step 3

← PULL

PULL →

Tighten each Overhand Knot individually, then pull on the standing parts so the knots slide together and lock.

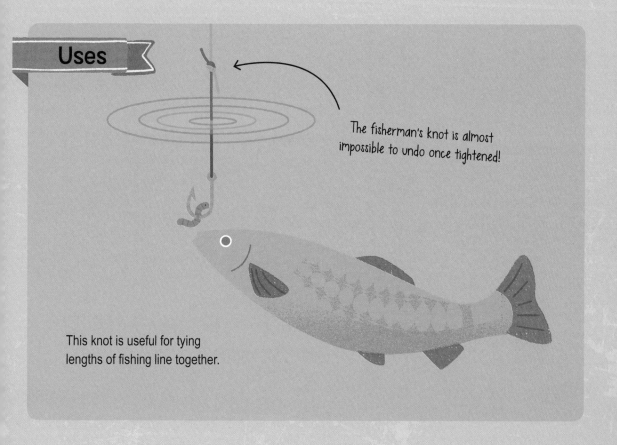

Uses

The fisherman's knot is almost impossible to undo once tightened!

This knot is useful for tying lengths of fishing line together.

Hunter's Bend

The hunter's bend is made up of two interlocked overhand knots. It is a good, reliable knot to use when joining two ropes or cords, but be careful—it can jam when pulled tightly and then become difficult to undo.

Step 1   Lay the two cords side by side, with the working ends in opposite directions, as shown.

Step 2

Take hold of both cords to the right of the middle and fold them over to the left to form a pair of loops.

The loop in the orange cord now sits on top and the loop in the yellow cord sits underneath. Take the working end of the top (orange) cord and thread it up through the middle of both loops.

Step 3

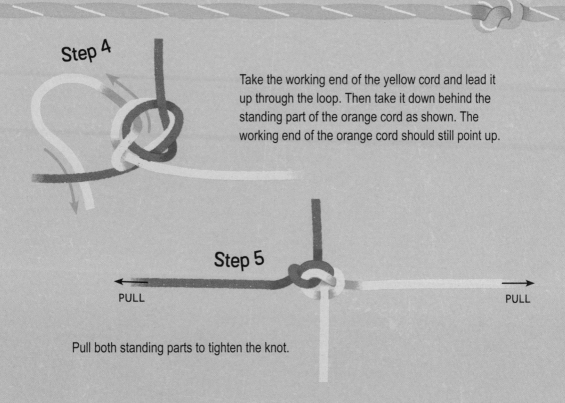

Step 4

Take the working end of the yellow cord and lead it up through the loop. Then take it down behind the standing part of the orange cord as shown. The working end of the orange cord should still point up.

Step 5

PULL

PULL

Pull both standing parts to tighten the knot.

Uses

Use a hunter's bend to securely tie two ropes together to create a tow rope.

The hunter's bend is one of the most secure bends you can use.

Sheet Bend

The sheet bend is a very old sailors' knot. It can be used to tie two lengths of rope together, and is very secure when pulled tight. The double version gives extra security, especially if the two ropes are different thicknesses.

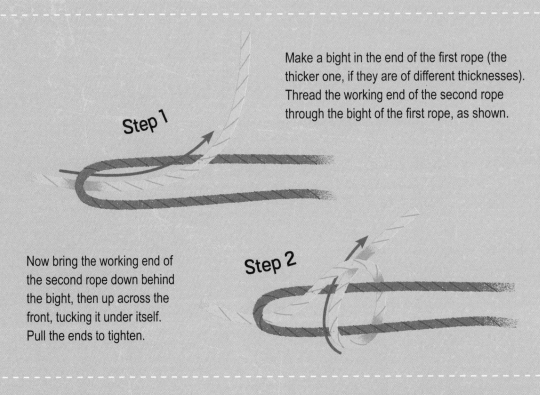

Make a bight in the end of the first rope (the thicker one, if they are of different thicknesses). Thread the working end of the second rope through the bight of the first rope, as shown.

Now bring the working end of the second rope down behind the bight, then up across the front, tucking it under itself. Pull the ends to tighten.

Double Sheet Bend

For a stronger knot, make the sheet bend as above, but wrap the second rope around the bight twice before tucking it under itself and tightening.

Wrap the rope around the bight twice.

Slipped Sheet Bend

This knot is useful because it is strong but can be quickly undone by pulling on the end of the rope that has been tucked under. It is ideal as a temporary bend.

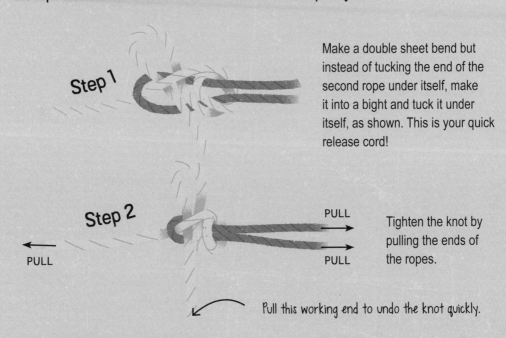

Step 1

Make a double sheet bend but instead of tucking the end of the second rope under itself, make it into a bight and tuck it under itself, as shown. This is your quick release cord!

Step 2

PULL

PULL

PULL

PULL

Tighten the knot by pulling the ends of the ropes.

Pull this working end to undo the knot quickly.

Uses

Fix a broken shoelace with this knot!

Use the slipped sheet bend as a quick fix for frayed or broken shoelaces. Lengthen your laces by simply tying on an extra piece of string.

Lapp Knot

This relative of the sheet bend has been used in the far north for a long time. It is easy to create and not too fiddly, which is good news for cold fingers! Pay attention to the direction of the ends when tying the lapp knot—both standing parts need to be on the same side of the knot.

Step 1

Take the end of the first rope and fold it back to form a bight, like this.

Step 2

Feed the working end of the second rope over and round the bight. Then take the working end back across itself and tuck it through the bight of the first rope. Pull the ends to tighten.

The standing parts are both on the same side of the knot.

Slipped Lapp Knot

PULL BOTH ENDS OF THE FIRST ROPE TO TIGHTEN

Uses

This easy, quick-release knot is very handy!

Hang items from a backpack by making a sling with the slipped Lapp Knot for instant access.

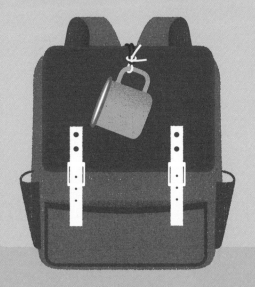

Create a Lapp knot, as above. Before tightening, make a bight in the second rope by feeding the working end back through the bight of the first rope.

Water Knot

The water knot is a bend specially designed to join flat material, such as two straps or tapes.

Step 1

Tie a loose overhand knot (page 6) near to the working end of the first strap.

Step 2

Now take the second strap and thread its working end back through the overhand knot. Trace the path of the first strap until the working end of the second strap emerges alongside the standing part of the first strap. If the knot is going to be used with a heavy load, make sure that the two working ends are at least several inches long.

Uses

This knot is handy for fixing a broken strap.

Step 3

Tighten the knot carefully.

Zeppelin Bend

This knot is made up of two interlocked overhand knots and gets its name because it was said to have been used to tie down large airships, such as the Zeppelin, back in the 1930s. The Zeppelin bend can be used to join ropes of different sizes and material and is a very secure knot that is easy to undo. It is therefore considered one of the best bends available!

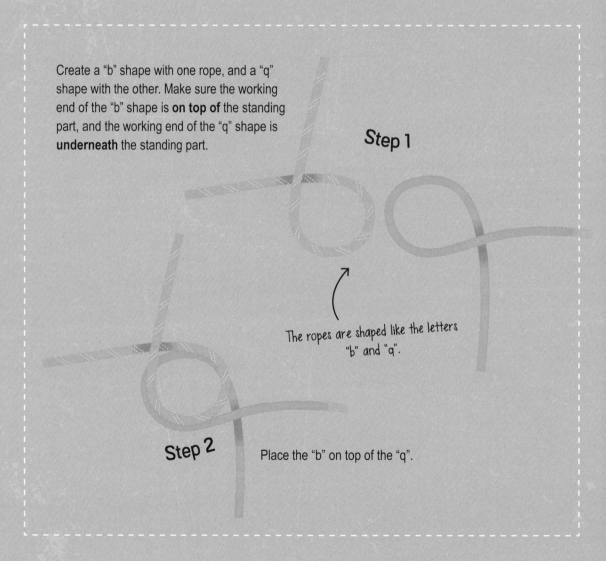

Create a "b" shape with one rope, and a "q" shape with the other. Make sure the working end of the "b" shape is **on top of** the standing part, and the working end of the "q" shape is **underneath** the standing part.

Step 1

The ropes are shaped like the letters "b" and "q".

Step 2

Place the "b" on top of the "q".

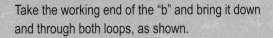

Take the working end of
the "q" and bring it up
and through both loops,
as shown.

Step 3

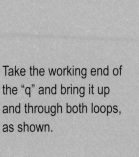

Step 4

Take the working end of the "b" and bring it down
and through both loops, as shown.

Step 5

To tighten the knot, pull evenly on the working ends and standing parts.

If the knot loosens, it can be easily be tightened by pulling on the standing parts.

For ropes of different thicknesses

Make the knot as in Steps 1 to 4, but use the thicker rope to form the letter "b". Before fully tightening the knot, take the working end of the thinner rope around the loop of the "b", again following its own path back up through the knot.

Step 1

Step 2

Pull carefully on all ends to tighten the knot.

Uses

This is a good knot for towing a car, as it is very secure but also easy to undo—even after it's been used to pull a heavy load.

Along with the hunter's bend, the Zeppelin bend is one of the most secure bends you can use.

CHAPTER 2: HITCHES

A hitch is a type of knot that is used to attach rope or cord to another object—or sometimes to another rope. There are many different types of hitches to try.

Some hitches are designed to attach a rope to a pole or another rope where the force applied is along the rope or pole at a very slight angle. These knots can be moved by sliding them along, but they will grip once pulled on tightly.

Half Hitch

The simple half hitch is usually a step in the tying of other knots, such as the round turn & two half hitches (page 27) and the buntline hitch (page 34).

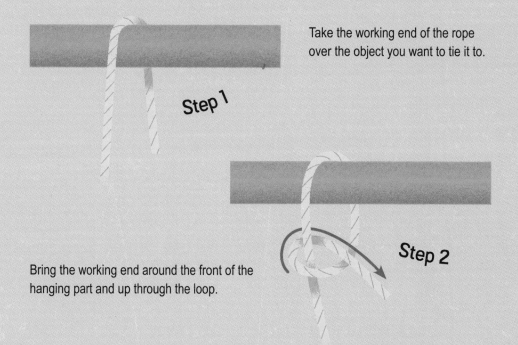

Take the working end of the rope over the object you want to tie it to.

Step 1

Bring the working end around the front of the hanging part and up through the loop.

Step 2

Round Turn & Two Half Hitches

This is a classic hitch that is strong, secure, reliable—and easy to remember! The extra loop over the rail means that some of the load is taken up by friction. Loosen the knot slightly and you will see that the free end is actually a clove hitch (page 36).

Step 1

Loop the working end of the rope twice over the rail, or whatever the hitch is to be attached to, leading to the right. This complete loop is known as a round turn.

Step 2

Use the working end to tie a half hitch around the hanging part of rope.

Step 3

Tie a second half hitch below the first one. Both half hitches should go in the same direction, with the working end leading to the right.

Step 4

PULL

PULL

Tighten by first pulling on the working end, then pull on the hanging part and slide the knot up to the rail.

Uses

A round turn & two half hitches works for anything from tethering an animal to setting up a washing line.

Anchor Hitch

Although this is also known as the fisherman's bend, this knot is actually a hitch and not a bend, which is confusing! The old name probably arises from sailors "bending a rope" onto something. It is more secure than a round turn & two half hitches and can be used on a small boat anchor. There are two ways to complete this knot.

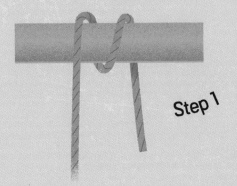

Loop the working end of the rope twice over the rail to make a round turn.

Step 1

Take the working end across the front of the hanging part of the rope and thread it through the underside of the loops. This makes a half hitch, but trapped by the loops around the rail. Tighten by pulling on both ends.

PULL

Step 2

PULL

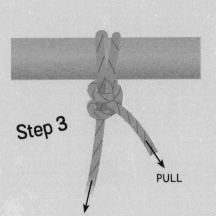

Step 3

PULL

PULL

With the working end, tie a second half hitch around the rope of the hanging part. Pull both ends to tighten, making sure the knot is pressed close to the rail.

Alternative Ending

Some people prefer to finish this knot by pushing the working end though the loops for a second time. This makes the knot more secure.

Uses

Fasten the standing part of a rope with this hitch when tying down luggage on a roof rack.

Becket Hitch

The becket hitch is very similar to the sheet bend, but rather than joining the ends of two lines, it is used to join a line to a loop. If the ropes are of different types or size, then the becket hitch can be doubled or tied in a different way for a more secure attachment.

Step 1

Feed the working end of the cord up through the loop from the right, then drop it over the back of the loop.

An overhand knot tied at the end of the cord will help stop it slip.

Now take the working end up and back over the loop, and under itself. If the knot is to be doubled, simply repeat this step.

Step 2

Secure Method

Pass the working end of the cord up through the loop, then around the back of the loop and down through the loop again.

Step 1

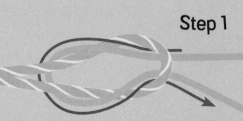

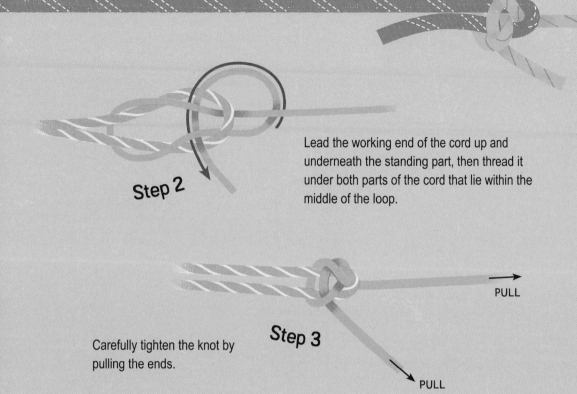

Step 2

Lead the working end of the cord up and underneath the standing part, then thread it under both parts of the cord that lie within the middle of the loop.

Step 3

PULL

PULL

Carefully tighten the knot by pulling the ends.

Uses

Use the becket hitch to join a cord to the sling on a tool handle, so you can carry it over your shoulder.

Blake's Hitch

A relatively new knot, this hitch is named after a Californian arborist called James Blake. An arborist is someone whose job is to take care of trees. Blake first explained this knot to other arborists in 1994, and it became a popular knot to use when ascending and descending trees.

Step 1

Take the working end of the thinner cord over the rope and loosely wind it around four times, going from right to left, as shown.

The cord used to make a Blake's Hitch should be thinner than the rope it is tied to.

Step 2

Lead the working end of the cord across to the right, in front of the hanging part.

Step 3

Now, feed the working end up and through the first two loops of the cord, to emerge from behind the rope.

PULL

Step 4

Tighten the knot carefully before use. If this knot is being used in a critical situation, add an overhand knot or figure 8 knot to the working end, to prevent it slipping through the knot.

PULL

Uses

This hitch is often used by tree surgeons as a "slide-and-grip" knot to attach two ropes. It also makes a heavy-duty adjustable loop for a tent's guy line.

Buntline Hitch

This old sailing knot was originally used to tie the foot of a square sail to its buntlines (a buntline is a vertical rope used to pull a sail up to furl it when not in use). As strong winds flapped the sails, the knot would conveniently tighten rather than loosen, making it even more secure. The downside of the buntline hitch is that it can jam under a heavy load.

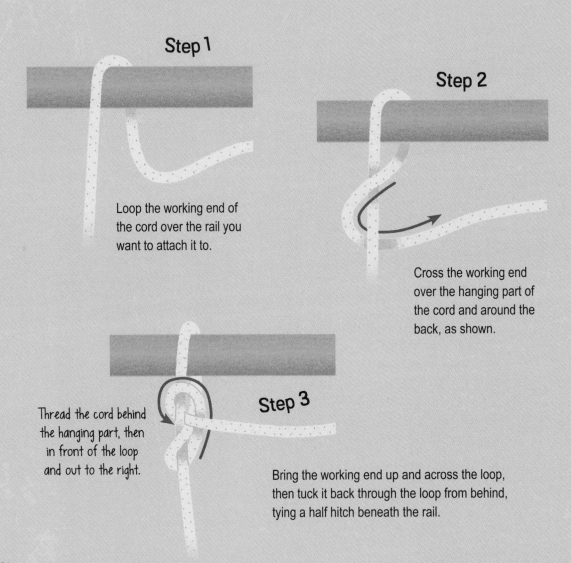

Step 1

Loop the working end of the cord over the rail you want to attach it to.

Step 2

Cross the working end over the hanging part of the cord and around the back, as shown.

Step 3

Thread the cord behind the hanging part, then in front of the loop and out to the right.

Bring the working end up and across the loop, then tuck it back through the loop from behind, tying a half hitch beneath the rail.

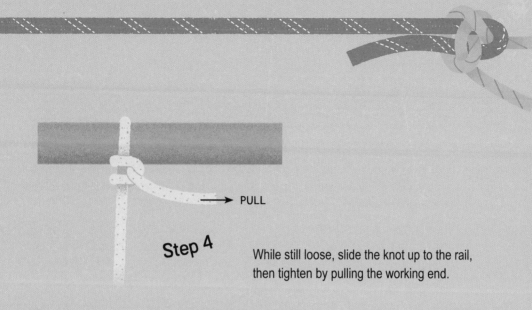

PULL

Step 4

While still loose, slide the knot up to the rail, then tighten by pulling the working end.

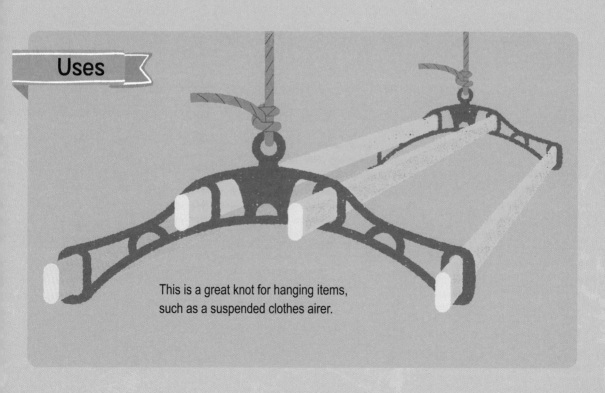

Uses

This is a great knot for hanging items, such as a suspended clothes airer.

Clove Hitch

The clove hitch is another very old knot that was used at sea. It is what is known as a "mid-line" knot, used to attach the middle of a length of rope to another rope, stake, or whatever.

An easy knot to tie, the clove hitch can be used to hold a series of posts in a line, ideally with a more secure hitch, such as a gnat hitch or half hitch, being used on the first and final posts in the line. The clove hitch can slip or come undone if the object it is tied to is rotated or doesn't maintain even pressure, which is why it's best to use other hitches for the end posts.

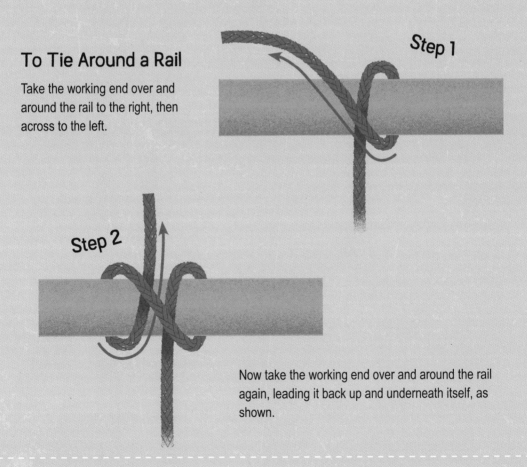

To Tie Around a Rail

Take the working end over and around the rail to the right, then across to the left.

Step 1

Step 2

Now take the working end over and around the rail again, leading it back up and underneath itself, as shown.

To Tie in Hand

This method works where the completed knot can be dropped over the end of a post—it can't be used around a rail if the end of the rail cannot be accessed.

Step 1

Make a loop in the rope as shown.

Make sure the direction of the loops are the same.

Step 2

Now, make a second loop in the same way as the first.

Step 3

Place the second loop behind the first loop. The knot is now ready to be placed over a post.

Uses

Link a series of canes or temporary fencing with clove hitches that can be easily adjusted.

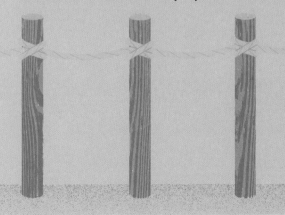

Cow Hitch

The cow hitch gets its name, quite simply, from being used to tether an cow to a post so it could graze in a circle. It's a quick and easy knot to learn and is fairly reliable as long as both ends hold weight, otherwise it will slip. It can be locked with a simple tuck, in which case one end should be left short.

Where Only One Rope End Is Available

Step 1

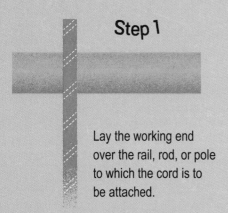

Lay the working end over the rail, rod, or pole to which the cord is to be attached.

Step 2

Take the working end over and around the rail to the left, then back across the cord and under the rail to the right.

Step 3

Bring the working end back over the rail and down under itself to complete the knot. Pull both ends to tighten.

Where Both Rope Ends Are Available

Make a bight in the cord, place the bight over the rail and tuck both ends through this bight. Pull both ends to tighten.

To Lock the Cow Hitch

Start with a cow hitch, with the working end quite short.

Step 1

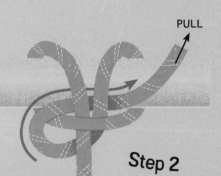

PULL

Step 2

PULL

Take the working end left, behind the hanging part, then thread it over the top of the bight (through which the ends go), passing behind both ends. Tighten the knot by pulling both ends.

Uses

A locked cow hitch is a good choice to tether an animal to a post.

Draw Hitch

The draw hitch is a "fast getaway" hitch. It is a secure fastening to a rail, yet with a sharp tug on the end of the rope it comes loose. Use it where a quick release may be required in an emergency.

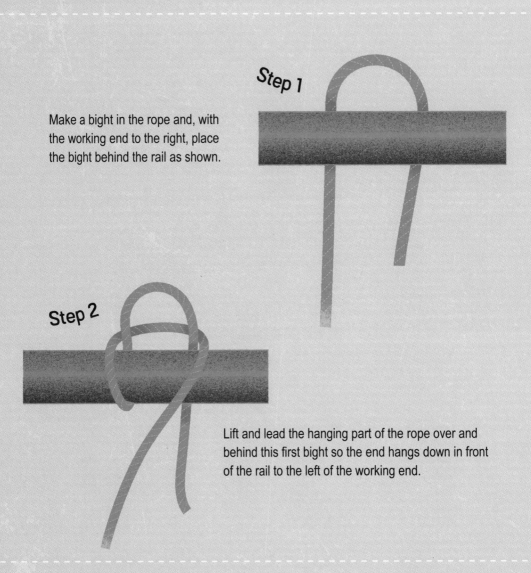

Step 1

Make a bight in the rope and, with the working end to the right, place the bight behind the rail as shown.

Step 2

Lift and lead the hanging part of the rope over and behind this first bight so the end hangs down in front of the rail to the left of the working end.

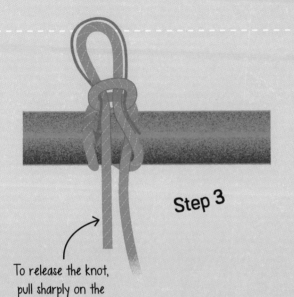

Step 3

Finally, make a bight in the working end of the rope and pass it up in front of the rail. Position it inside the first bight, over the hanging part of the rope. Carefully tighten the knot by pulling on the hanging part.

To release the knot, pull sharply on the working end.

Uses

Thread the rope through a tool handle during Step 3 and hang it from a rail for instant access.

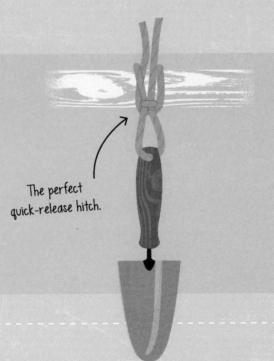

The perfect quick-release hitch.

Gnat Hitch

Easy and quick to tie as well as being secure, the gnat hitch is a relatively new knot—it was first documented in 2012. It does a similar job to the buntline hitch, but is easier to tie. It has good grip and is jam-resistant unless it is pulled very tight.

Lead the rope over the rail and tie a half hitch around the hanging part of the rope, as shown.

Step 1

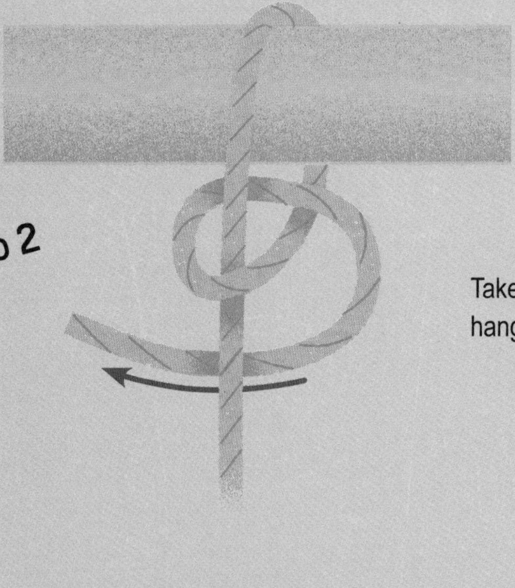

Step 2

Take the working end behind the hanging part and to the left.

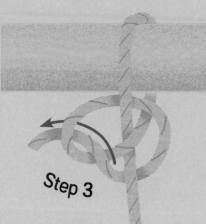

Step 3

Now tuck the working end down through the loop of the half hitch, to the left of the hanging part.

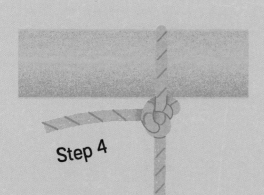

Step 4

Tighten the knot, then pull on the hanging part to slide the knot up against the rail.

PULL TO SLIDE
THE KNOT UP

Uses

The gnat hitch is used by gardeners to attach string to canes or hang a bird feeder from a branch.

Ground Line Hitch

This is a neat and simple little hitch for attaching a rope to a rail, pole, or a thicker rope at right angles. Fishermen use it to attach nets and lobster pots to the main rope.

When used as a hitch for attaching the end of a rope to a rail or pole, it is better than the clove hitch as it is more secure and less likely to jam. However, it will only work if the pole is cylindrical.

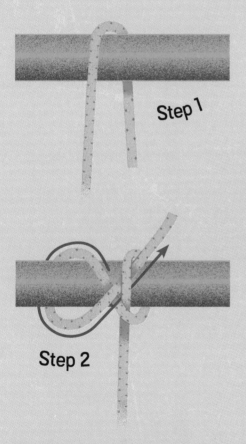

Step 1

Loop the rope over the rail, as shown.

Step 2

Take the working end across the hanging part to the left, around the rail, then back across itself. Tuck the free end under the hanging part of the rope and tighten.

Uses

This is a good knot for hanging boat fenders. It can also be used by gardeners to tie a string to bamboo canes.

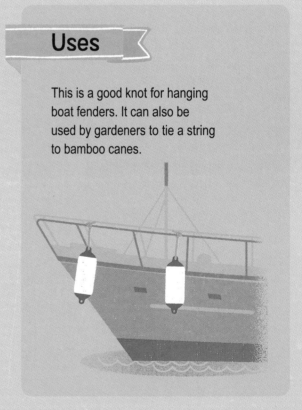

Pipe Hitch

The pipe hitch is used to pull or lift a cylindrical pole, such as scaffolding. It can also be used to attach a rope to a pole where the pull is along the length of the pole.

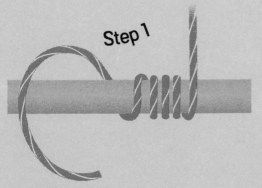

Step 1

Wrap the working end of the rope around the pole at least four times. The number of wraps depends on how heavy and slippery the pole is—add more wraps if you are unsure.

Step 2

Take the working end back to the standing part and tie two Half Hitches around the standing part, one above the other, where the first wrap starts, as shown.

Always test whether there's enough support before raising or lowering a heavy pole, and add more wraps if needed.

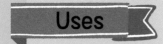
Uses

The pipe hitch can be used to hang tools with a smooth handle, such as a rake.

Knute Hitch

This simple hitch is a useful one to know. It is used to attach a cord to a tool or anything with a hole in the handle. Attached in seconds and released just as quickly, this is a very handy way to hang something.

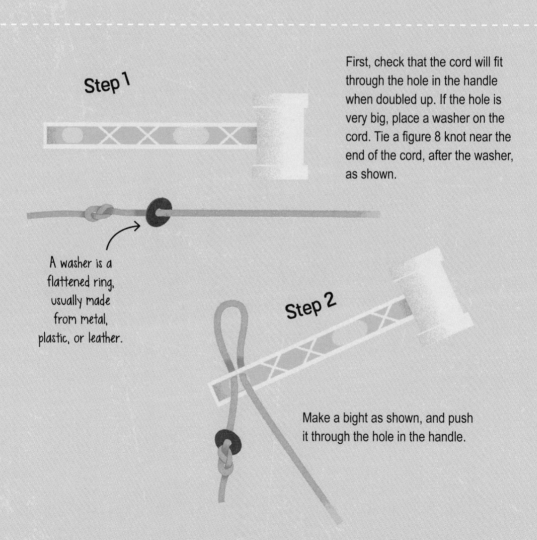

Step 1

First, check that the cord will fit through the hole in the handle when doubled up. If the hole is very big, place a washer on the cord. Tie a figure 8 knot near the end of the cord, after the washer, as shown.

A washer is a flattened ring, usually made from metal, plastic, or leather.

Step 2

Make a bight as shown, and push it through the hole in the handle.

Step 3

Bring the figure 8 knot and washer either around the side of the handle or over the top, then feed it through the bight.

Step 4

Pull tight on the standing part. To remove the tool, loosen the cord and push the figure 8 knot back through the bight.

PULL TO TIGHTEN

Uses

This hitch can be used to attach rope to the eyelets of a tarpaulin for easy removal without undoing any knots.

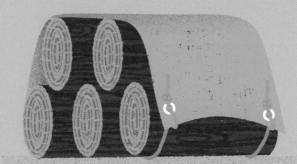

Marlinspike Hitch

This simple noose took its name from a marlinspike, a tool used by sailors for working with ropes. It is used to attach a marlinspike, hammer, or other tool to a cord or rope in order to make a handle. It is also a good choice of knot to tie around wooden rungs to make a rope ladder.

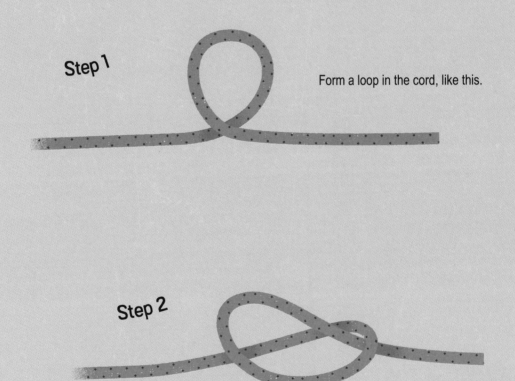

Step 1

Form a loop in the cord, like this.

Step 2

Hold the top of the loop and fold it down over the left-hand section of cord.

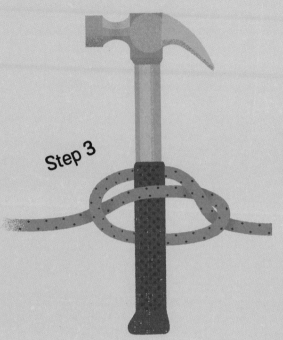

Step 3

Insert the hammer, or other item, into the knot by threading it under the middle part of the cord, but on top of the loop. Hold the hammer steady and pull the ends to tighten.

Uses

Use with a hammer, screwdriver, or other cylindrical item to create a handle to drag something heavy, such as a log.

Pile Hitch and Double Pile Hitch

This hitch is very easy to tie, yet very secure, and is often used to moor a boat. The hitch is created in the middle of the rope, so it's a handy knot to know if the ends of the rope are out of reach or inaccessible. The pile hitch is not possible where the end of whatever it is being tied to is not available, e.g. a floor-to-ceiling pole. If the line is slippery, use a double pile hitch instead.

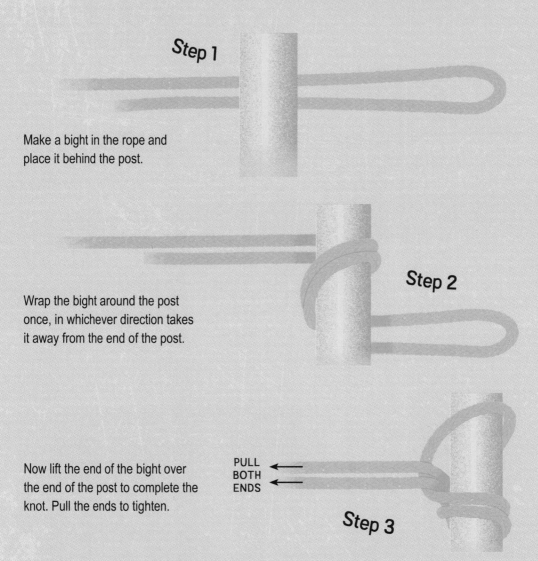

Step 1

Make a bight in the rope and place it behind the post.

Step 2

Wrap the bight around the post once, in whichever direction takes it away from the end of the post.

Now lift the end of the bight over the end of the post to complete the knot. Pull the ends to tighten.

PULL BOTH ENDS ←

Step 3

To Tie a Double Pile Hitch

After Step 2, wrap the bight around the post once more before moving onto Step 3.

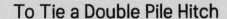

Wrapping the rope
an extra time helps
prevent slipping.

![Uses] The pile hitch can be used as a temporary boat mooring, as it is very easy to cast on and off.

Prusik Knot

In 1931, Dr. Karl Prusik, a mountaineer from Austria, demonstrated the Prusik Knot. Since then it has become a commonly used knot in sports such as climbing, caving, and abseiling. It is used to tie a loop of cord, also known as a sling, around a vertical rope. The knot can slide up and down easily, but locks in place when bearing weight.

As well as being used in sports, the Prusik Knot is also useful for making a "rope handle" on a vertical rope, e.g. to hang a hook with a tool bag.

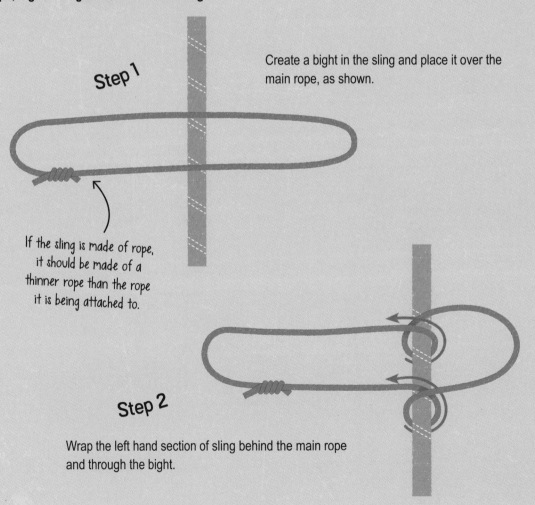

Step 1

Create a bight in the sling and place it over the main rope, as shown.

If the sling is made of rope, it should be made of a thinner rope than the rope it is being attached to.

Step 2

Wrap the left hand section of sling behind the main rope and through the bight.

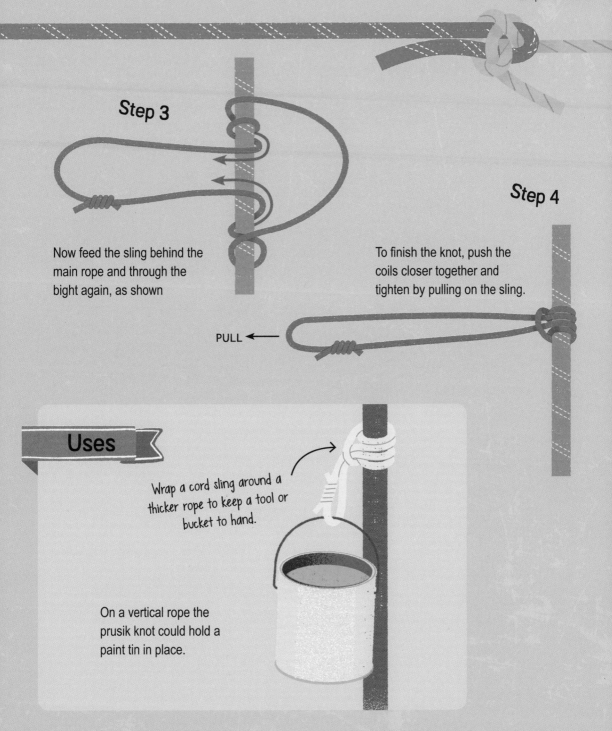

Step 3

Now feed the sling behind the main rope and through the bight again, as shown

Step 4

To finish the knot, push the coils closer together and tighten by pulling on the sling.

PULL ←

Uses

Wrap a cord sling around a thicker rope to keep a tool or bucket to hand.

On a vertical rope the prusik knot could hold a paint tin in place.

Rolling Hitch

The rolling hitch can be used to attach a rope to a smooth pole, e.g. scaffolding, where the load will be along the pole. It can also be used to attach one rope to another. This hitch can be slid along by hand to adjust the position of the attaching rope, but will grip when pulled tightly. It has a tendency to slip with modern ropes, so use it carefully in this instance.

To Tie the Rolling Hitch to a Solid Pole

Step 1

Wrap the working end around the pole at least twice, as shown.

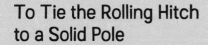

If the pole or cord is slippery, add more turns.

PULL

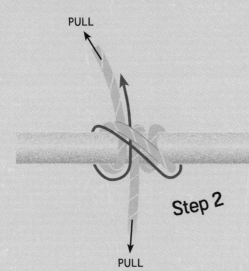

Step 2

PULL

Take the working end across the front of the pole and wrapped cord and tie a half hitch to the left of the hanging part. Pull on both ends and tighten the knot well before applying load.

To Tie the Rolling Hitch to a Rope

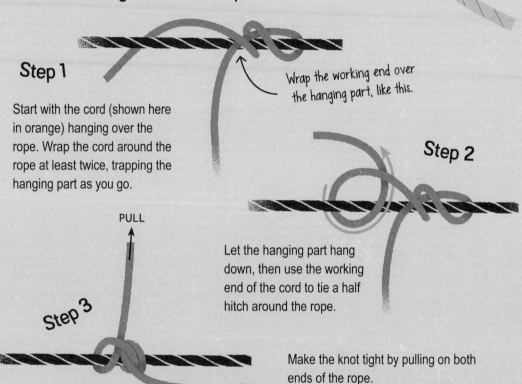

Step 1

Start with the cord (shown here in orange) hanging over the rope. Wrap the cord around the rope at least twice, trapping the hanging part as you go.

Wrap the working end over the hanging part, like this.

Step 2

Let the hanging part hang down, then use the working end of the cord to tie a half hitch around the rope.

Step 3

PULL

PULL

Make the knot tight by pulling on both ends of the rope.

Uses

A rolling hitch can be used to attach a line to a rope when towing a dinghy.

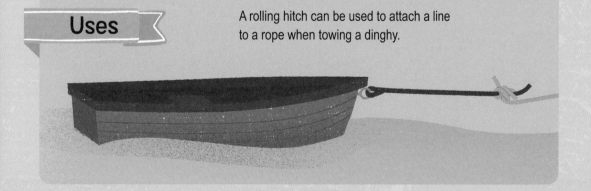

Tensionless Hitch

This knot is often used in rescue situations, but is also very useful for tasks such as hanging a swing—especially a monkey swing from the branch of a tree. It is very simple to tie but does need to be used with a large shackle or a carabiner.

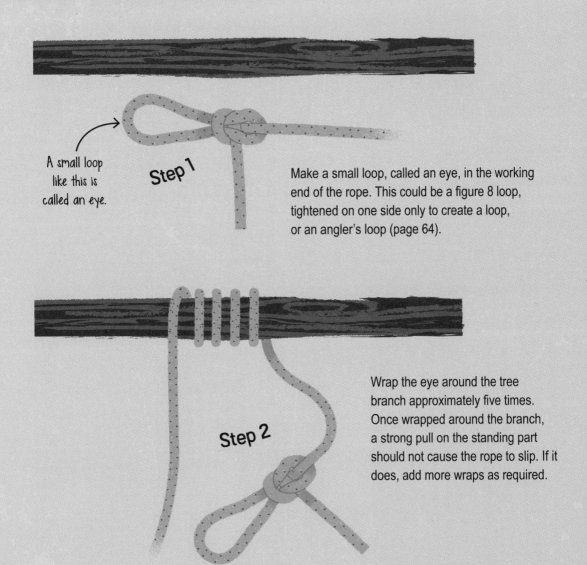

A small loop like this is called an eye.

Step 1

Make a small loop, called an eye, in the working end of the rope. This could be a figure 8 loop, tightened on one side only to create a loop, or an angler's loop (page 64).

Step 2

Wrap the eye around the tree branch approximately five times. Once wrapped around the branch, a strong pull on the standing part should not cause the rope to slip. If it does, add more wraps as required.

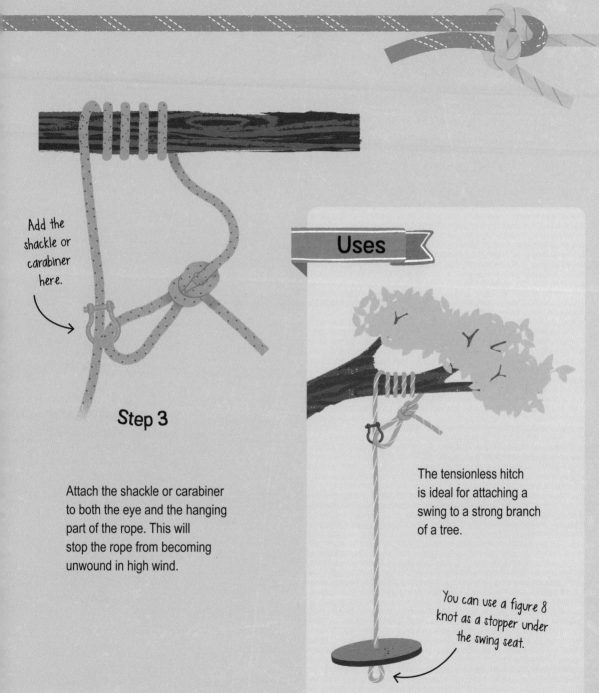

Add the shackle or carabiner here.

Step 3

Attach the shackle or carabiner to both the eye and the hanging part of the rope. This will stop the rope from becoming unwound in high wind.

Uses

The tensionless hitch is ideal for attaching a swing to a strong branch of a tree.

You can use a figure 8 knot as a stopper under the swing seat.

Timber Hitch

This handy, secure noose is easy to make, simple to undo and cannot jam. It's called a timber hitch because it was devised in order to pull large logs. It is also used to attach strings on some stringed instruments, such as the guitar and ukulele.

Step 1

Take the working end over the log from behind, then cross it in front of the hanging part. Thread it back through the loop just formed, as shown.

Step 2

A noose is a loop that can easily be adjusted in size.

Wrap the working end back around the loop multiple times. The hanging part will now run through a small eye, making a noose.

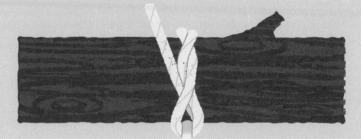

When the hanging rope is pulled, the noose will tighten and the wraps will be trapped against the log.

Step 3

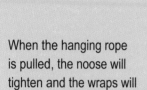

Uses

Use this hitch when pruning trees. Attach a rope to the branch you want to prune. Once tied, lead the rope over a higher branch and tether to a solid object on the ground. Cut branches can be then be lowered safely by releasing tension on the rope.

CHAPTER 3: LOOPS, KNOTS & NOOSES

This chapter covers adjustable and fixed-size loops. Slings, which are loops formed by joining the two ends of a rope, are also included, though the knots for joining the ends to create the loop are usually bends. Nooses, which can be adjusted in size, are sometimes referred to as slip knots. But don't confuse a slip knot with a slipped knot—they are quite different!

Overhand Loop

This is a simple but secure loop that is difficult to undo once it has been pulled very tight. The overhand loop can also be tied near to the end of a line to form a reliable stopper knot.

The overhand loop is better in string than rope, because it does jam tightly.

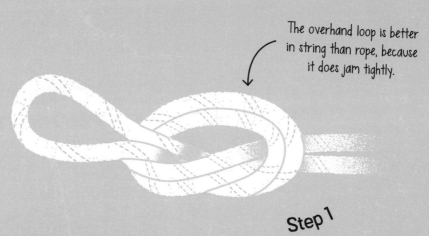

Step 1

Double-up the cord to make a bight. Tie an overhand knot in the doubled cord, so that the bight emerges to form a loop at the end.

Step 2

← PULL

PULL →

Tighten by pulling the loop away
from the doubled cord.

Uses

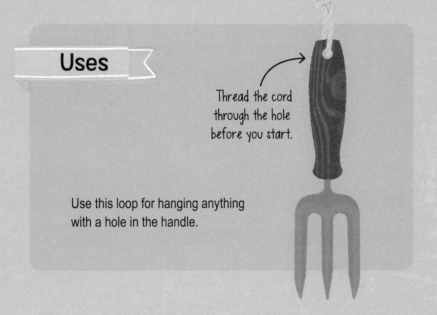

Thread the cord
through the hole
before you start.

Use this loop for hanging anything
with a hole in the handle.

Figure 8 Loop

The figure 8 loop is tied the same way as the figure 8 knot on page 7, but using a doubled cord. There are two ways of tying this loop—use whichever you find easiest.

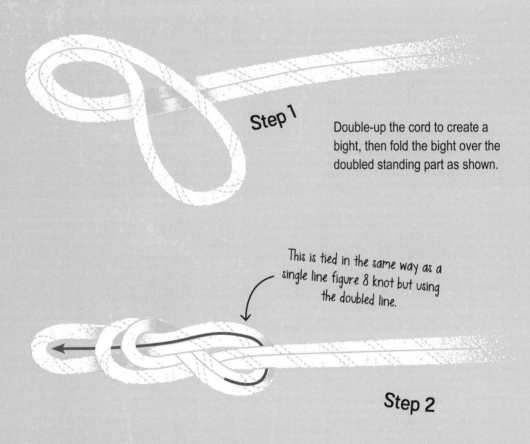

Step 1

Double-up the cord to create a bight, then fold the bight over the doubled standing part as shown.

This is tied in the same way as a single line figure 8 knot but using the doubled line.

Step 2

Wrap the bight under the doubled standing part, and back through the loop formed by the doubled cord.

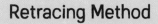

Retracing Method

Start with a simple, single-line figure 8 knot. With the working end, retrace the knot, keeping the cords side by side, to form the loop.

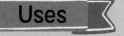

Uses

This is a strong loop that works well in the end of stiff material. You can attach a vehicle tow rope to a ring or towbar by using the retracing method above.

Angler's Loop

Also known as the perfection loop, this is an old fishing knot that can be used with modern synthetic line. It is secure but it can jam if it is tied very tightly, so only use it when untying is not needed. It works well with standard string or cord, and also with stretchy cord—unlike most loop knots.

There are two methods of tying this loop. Method 1 is very easy if you need a loop at the end of a cord. Method 2 can be used to make the loop around an object or through a ring.

Method 1

Step 1

Make a bight in the rope with the working end to the left. Take the working end under the standing part and back over the bight to form a larger loop to the right.

The size of this loop determines how big the loop in the final knot will be.

Step 2

Take the working end and wrap it around the top of the original bight.

PULL

Step 3

Take the larger loop from the right and pass it up through the front of the original bight. Pull the loop and both ends to tighten the knot.

PULL

PULL

Method 2

Step 1

Make a simple overhand knot in the rope at the point where the final knot is needed. Note that this knot is formed by going under first, then over.

Step 2

Feed the working end through the object to which the loop is to be attached (such as a ring) and back through the loop of the overhand knot, making a slip knot.

Step 3

Lead the working end underneath the hanging part and squeeze it through the overhand knot, as shown.

PULL

Step 4

Finally, feed the working end underneath itself, as shown. Pull the loop and hanging part of the rope to tighten the knot.

PULL

Uses

This knot will make a secure loop in elasticated cord for use on a trailer with fixing hooks on the side.

Common Bowline

Also known simply as the bowline, pronounced "*bo-lin*", this is known as the "king of knots", probably because it has been used at sea for hundreds of years. It is simple to tie and won't jam. It is easy to untie, as long as it is not under load. The common bowline can become loose, so for more secure versions, the Scott's lock (page 68), double bowline (page 70), and the water bowline (page 72) are good alternatives.

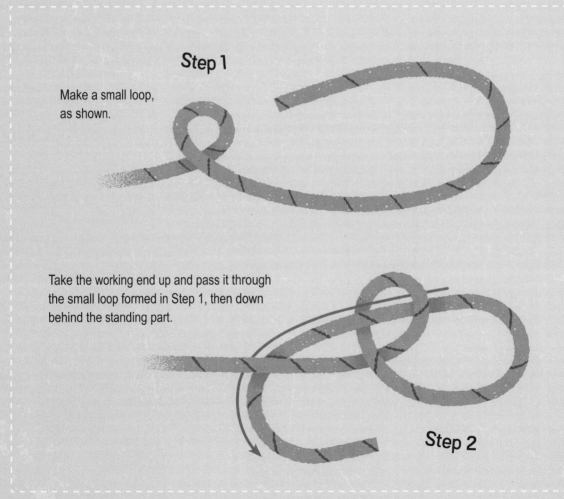

Step 1

Make a small loop, as shown.

Take the working end up and pass it through the small loop formed in Step 1, then down behind the standing part.

Step 2

Bring the working end back down through the small loop, following the same path as before. Tighten the knot carefully, keeping the working end inside the larger loop.

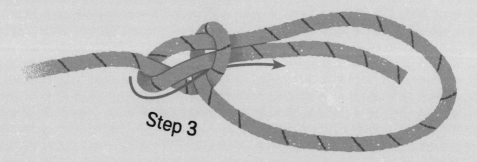

Step 3

Uses

The common bowline is a general purpose loop for use afloat or ashore. It's a good loop to use if you need to be able to untie it again easily.

Two bowlines can be used to join two separate ropes.

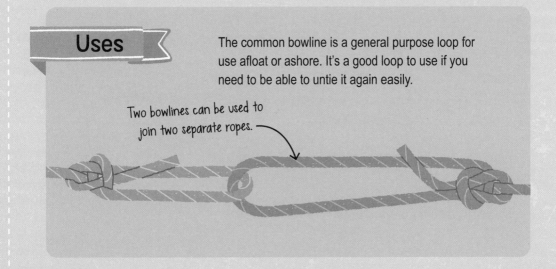

Scott's Lock

This was devised by Scott Safir, an American member of the International Guild of Knot Tyers. It is a simple addition to the common bowline that adds extra security.

Step 1

First tie a common bowline, but leave the knot loose.

This is the complete knot before it is tightened.

Step 2

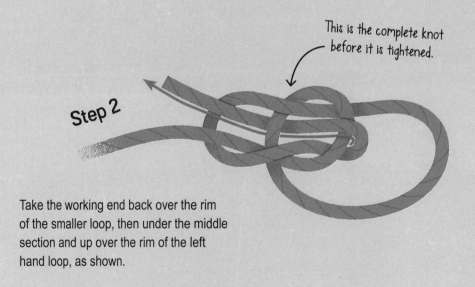

Take the working end back over the rim of the smaller loop, then under the middle section and up over the rim of the left hand loop, as shown.

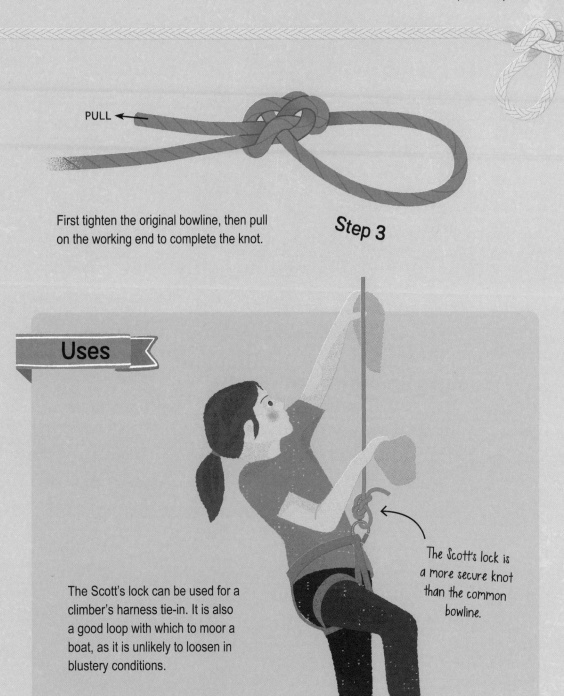

First tighten the original bowline, then pull on the working end to complete the knot.

Step 3

Uses

The Scott's lock can be used for a climber's harness tie-in. It is also a good loop with which to moor a boat, as it is unlikely to loosen in blustery conditions.

The Scott's lock is a more secure knot than the common bowline.

Double Bowline

This knot (also called the round turn bowline) is more secure than the common bowline and is very easy to tie. It has what is known as a double nipping loop, which provides more grip when you're working with stiff or slippery material.

Step 1

Start by making two overhand loops, one on top of the other, like this.

Step 2

Take the working end underneath and then through the middle of the loops made in Step 1.

Step 3

Now pass the working end underneath the standing part and back through the middle of the two loops, ending up inside the large loop on the right.

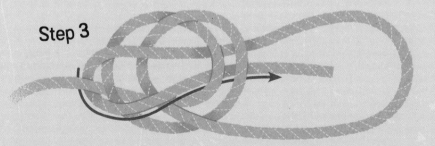

Tighten carefully by pulling on
both ends and the main loop.

Step 4

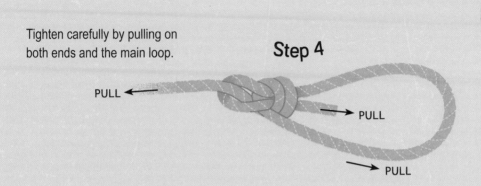

PULL ←

PULL →

PULL →

Uses

The double bowline provides a little more security than the
comon bowline, and is often used on a mooring rope.

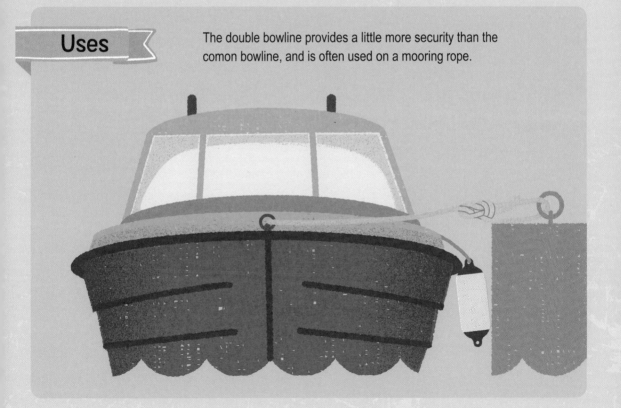

Water Bowline

The water bowline is so called because even after it has been in water, and the rope may have swollen, it is still easy to undo. This is another knot that offers more security than the common bowline.

Step 1

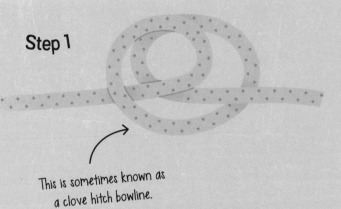

Make two overhand loops. Slide the second loop under the first to form a clove hitch (page 36).

This is sometimes known as a clove hitch bowline.

Step 2

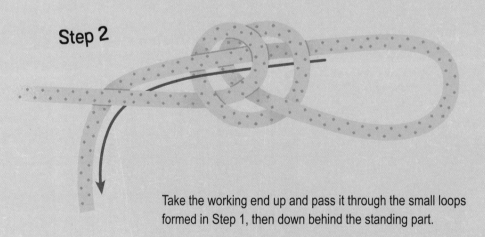

Take the working end up and pass it through the small loops formed in Step 1, then down behind the standing part.

Step 3

Thread the working end
back through both loops.

Under load the two loops of the clove hitch
may separate. This is to be expected and
does not mean that the knot is slipping.

Step 4

Carefully tighten the knot.

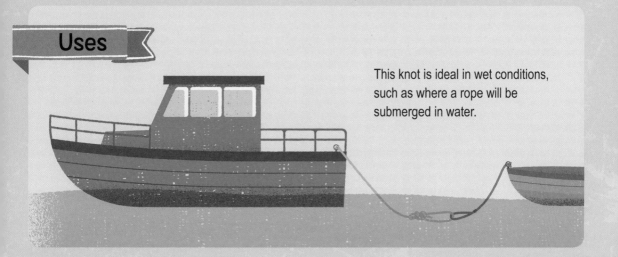

Uses

This knot is ideal in wet conditions,
such as where a rope will be
submerged in water.

Bowstring Knot

The bowstring knot is one of the simplest and also one of the oldest knots known. It is quick, simple to tie and surprisingly secure. Unlike other nooses that tighten when the rope is pulled, the bowstring knot loop gets bigger, so it can be used as a temporary dog collar and lead without chance of choking the animal.

Tie an overhand knot in the rope, exactly like this. You need to be able to make a loop from the length of rope in the working end, so don't tie the knot too close to the end.

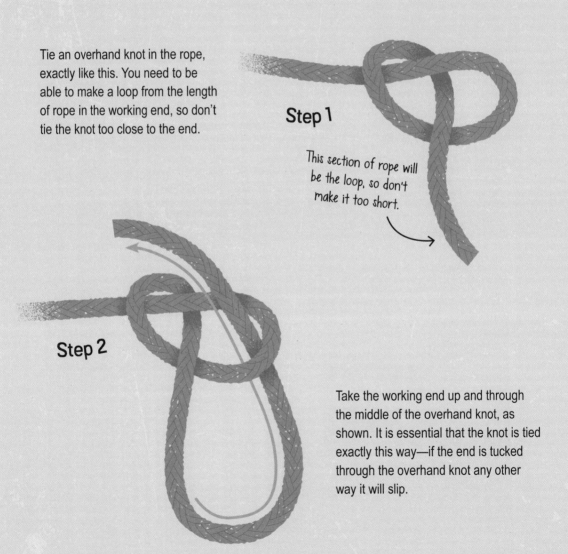

Step 1

This section of rope will be the loop, so don't make it too short.

Step 2

Take the working end up and through the middle of the overhand knot, as shown. It is essential that the knot is tied exactly this way—if the end is tucked through the overhand knot any other way it will slip.

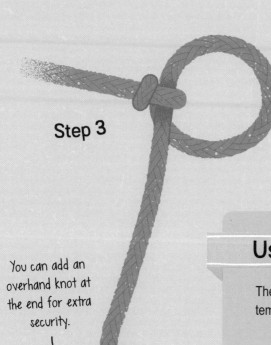

Step 3

You can add an
overhand knot at
the end for extra
security.

Tighten the overhand knot to trap the working end, forming a loop. This loop can be adjusted easily by pulling on the working end. Surprisingly, the working end does not easily slip if the loop is pulled on, but adding an overhand knot at the end of the working end will prevent it from slipping out completely.

Uses

The bowstring knot can be used to make a temporary dog collar and lead.

Butterfly Loop

Sometimes referred to as the alpine butterfly (because it was published in *The Alpine Journal* in the 1920s), this is a very secure and strong loop tied in the middle of a rope—the ends of the rope are not used. This knot will take a load in any direction.

Apart from its value as a loop, it can also be used to isolate a section of damaged rope. The knot can easily be tied around the hand and the size adjusted as it is tied.

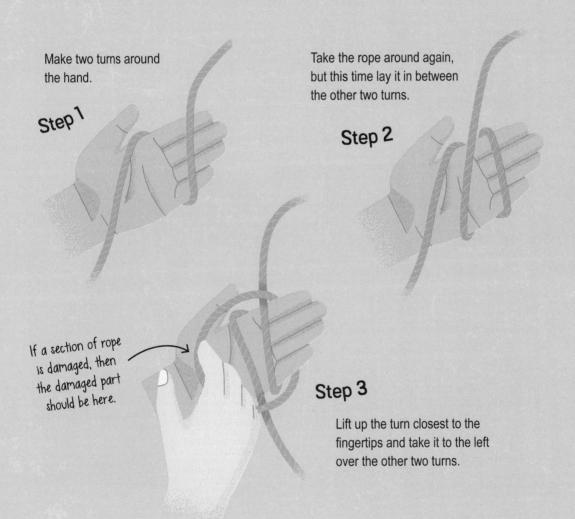

Make two turns around the hand.

Step 1

Take the rope around again, but this time lay it in between the other two turns.

Step 2

If a section of rope is damaged, then the damaged part should be here.

Step 3

Lift up the turn closest to the fingertips and take it to the left over the other two turns.

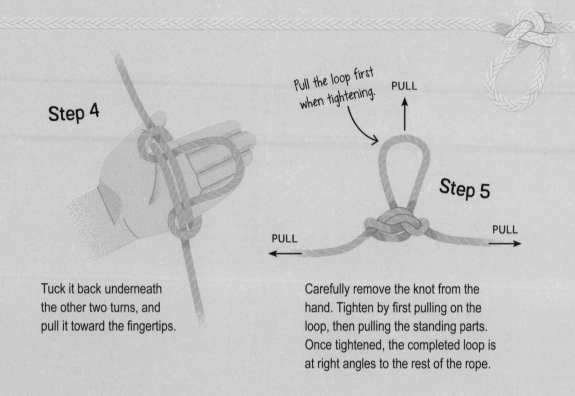

Step 4

Tuck it back underneath the other two turns, and pull it toward the fingertips.

Pull the loop first when tightening.

PULL

Step 5

PULL

PULL

Carefully remove the knot from the hand. Tighten by first pulling on the loop, then pulling the standing parts. Once tightened, the completed loop is at right angles to the rest of the rope.

Uses

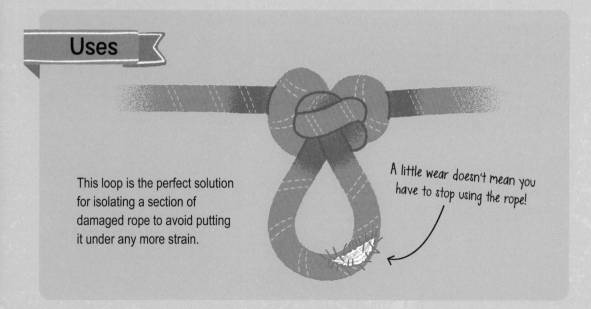

This loop is the perfect solution for isolating a section of damaged rope to avoid putting it under any more strain.

A little wear doesn't mean you have to stop using the rope!

Eskimo Bowline

This variation of a bowline was in use by Inuit people long before being discovered by the Arctic explorer Sir John Ross in the nineteenth century. Compared to a simple common bowline, this version is better at withstanding its loop being pulled outward. It is also easy to turn this into a slipped loop, as shown, so that it can be quickly undone.

Step 2

Take the working end down through the loop.

Step 1

Make a small loop in the cord.

Step 3

Lead the working end under the standing part and over to the right.

Step 4

Now take the working end back up through the first small loop you made and back out behind the bigger loop, as shown.

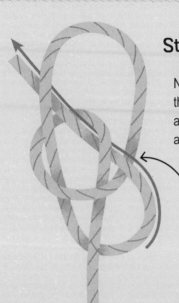

Make sure you lead the cord over, under, over, under, in that order.

Step 5

PULL

Tighten carefully, checking that one face of the knot looks like this.

PULL

Uses

Use the Eskimo bowline to moor to a large bollard, rather than the common bowline.

Farmer's Loop

This is another midline loop that is very easy and quick to tie around the hand. It is strong and secure too.

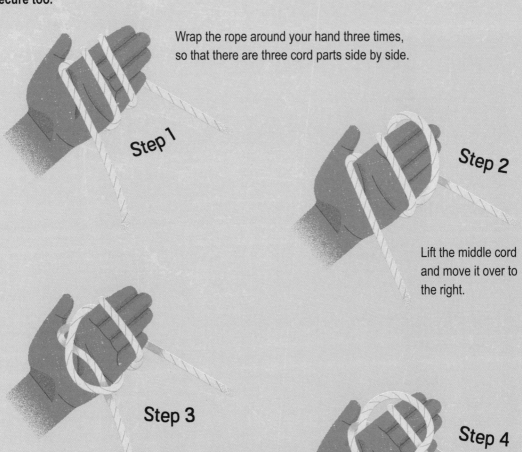

Wrap the rope around your hand three times, so that there are three cord parts side by side.

Step 1

Step 2

Lift the middle cord and move it over to the right.

Step 3

Lift the new middle cord and move it over to the left.

Step 4

Then lift the new middle cord and move it over to the right.

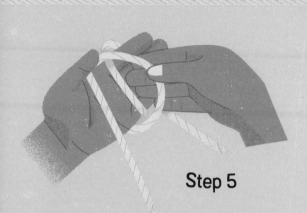

Step 5

Now lift the new middle cord up and away from your palm and slide your hand out of the rest of the cord. Pull on the loop you are holding and tighten the knot beneath it.

Step 6

This is the completed loop.

Remembering the Sequence

middle to right
middle to left
middle to right
middle goes up

Uses

The farmer's loop is useful for making a handhold, for hanging tools, or for shortening a longer rope.

Poacher's Noose

This is a noose knot that tightens as a load is hung below it. It grips well, though it will collapse unless there is something in the loop to stop it, such as a thimble. (A thimble is a plastic or metal object inserted into rope to stop it from wearing.) The noose is also useful for attaching a rope to a metal loop.

Step 1

Make a large bight in the working end. Take the working end up and over the standing part, as shown.

Step 2

Wrap the working end back around itself and the main length of rope twice, heading toward the loop. Keep the turns loose at this stage.

Thread the working end back through all the turns made in Step 2. Tighten the knot by pulling on the working end.

PULL

Step 3

If a thimble is to be used, insert it into the loop, as shown, before tightening. Support the thimble as you tighten the knot, so it doesn't slide out of position.

Step 4

A thimble will help the loop hold its position.

Adjust the loop to the size required by sliding the knot along the length of rope.

Uses

This can be used to weigh a tarpaulin down without an eyelet in place. Place a smooth stone under a section of the tarpaulin, then make the poacher's noose around it.

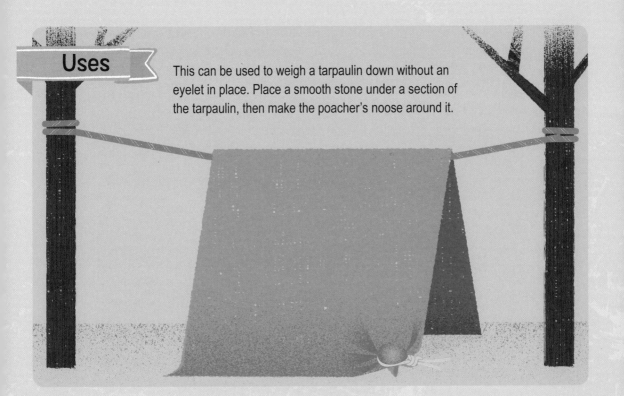

CHAPTER 4: BINDING KNOTS

A binding knot is tied around one or more objects to hold them together. This could be a bundle of sticks, a wrapped parcel, or a roll of carpet. It can also be used to hold a chair frame together while it is being glued.

Constrictor Knot

This binding knot is suitable for curved surfaces. It is ideal for tying around a bundle or, in an emergency, to hold a hosepipe to a tap.

There are two tying methods. The first is for tying the knot around something large, when you are able to use the working end. The second method is tied in your hand, mid-line, then placed over or around an object.

WARNING: A constrictor knot is very difficult to undo once it's been tightened and, like the strangle knot (page 92), it should never be tied around a part of the body.

To Tie Directly Around Something

Step 1

Loop the working end of your cord over the object, so it hangs to the right of the standing part. Then take it left across itself and around the object again, so it hangs down from behind.

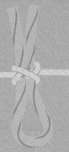

Lead the working end up and over the standing part, then thread it beneath the crossed cords at the top of the object. This forms an overhand knot, trapped underneath the wrapped cord.

Step 2

PULL

Step 3

The constrictor knot is simple, but very secure.

PULL

Pull both ends hard to tighten.

NOTE: See the marlinspike hitch (page 48) and pile hitch (page 50) for knots that can be used to attach two screwdrivers to the cord ends, creating handles that you can use to drag the object if heavy.

To Tie a Constrictor Knot in Hand

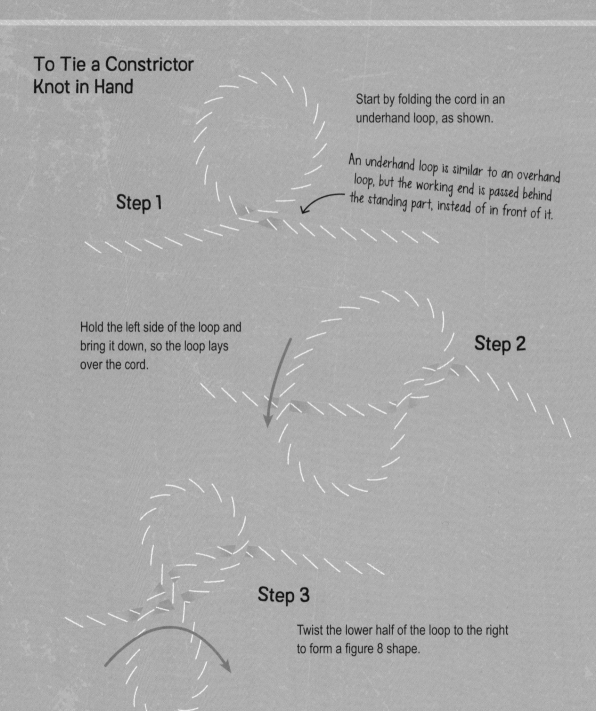

Start by folding the cord in an underhand loop, as shown.

An underhand loop is similar to an overhand loop, but the working end is passed behind the standing part, instead of in front of it.

Step 1

Hold the left side of the loop and bring it down, so the loop lays over the cord.

Step 2

Step 3

Twist the lower half of the loop to the right to form a figure 8 shape.

Step 4

Now fold the lower loop of the figure 8 under and upward, so that the loops are one on top of the other, like this.

PULL

Step 5

You have made a constrictor knot. Place the two loops around whatever is to be bound, then pull the ends to tighten.

PULL

Uses

This knot is a good choice for tying a bundle of cables or ropes together.

Gleipnir

The word "gleipnir" comes from Norse mythology and refers to the knot used to restrain the mighty wolf Fenrir. The gleipnir knot is simple but clever. It forms a binding around just about anything.

You will need a cord long enough to pass around the object twice, with enough left over to complete the knot.

Step 1

Double the cord and, with a finger in the bight, twist once.

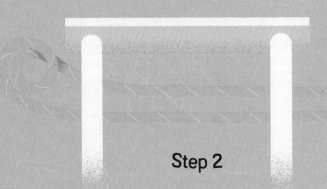

Fold the small loop back on itself and, holding this loop, place the doubled cord around the object or objects to be bound. The loop needs to be positioned close to the left edge of the object.

Step 2

Take one end of the cord and feed it behind and back through the loop. Feed the other end straight through the loop, so that the two ends now point away from each other.

Step 3

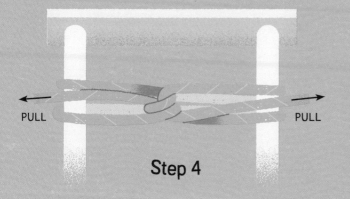

Step 4

PULL ←   → PULL

Pull the two ends in opposite directions to tighten the knot and lock it in place. To make the knot more secure, create a half hitch in each end around the doubled cord—although this may make the knot more difficult to undo later!

To Undo the Knot

If half hitches were added as suggested in Step 4, then these must be undone first. Then find the cord end that passes straight through the middle loop and pull it back through the knot. This will loosen the entire cord and release the knot.

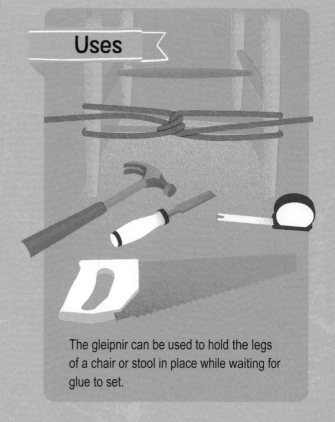

Uses

The gleipnir can be used to hold the legs of a chair or stool in place while waiting for glue to set.

Pole Lashing

The pole lashing is a handy way of tying a bundle of sticks, canes, or poles together. It's an easy knot to create, and simple to undo later.

Arrange the cord in a "N" shape, as shown.

Place the bundle of sticks or poles over the middle of the cord, like this.

Step 2

Step 1

Step 3

Feed each end through the bight on the opposite side of the bundle and pull the cord tight.

Tie the ends in a reef knot (page 94).

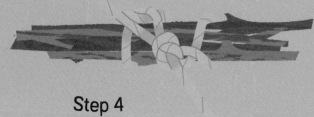

Step 4

(page 94).

Uses

Use the pole lashing to tie a bundle of sticks together, making them easier to carry.

The pole lashing is easy to undo after use.

Strangle Knot

The strangle knot is a binding knot for a rounded surface such as a rope or rail. It is also ideal for winding around the end of a rope to stop it fraying. Once tightened, it is very difficult to undo and may need to be cut off for removal. Unlike the similar constrictor knot (page 84), the ends emerge from the sides of the knot rather than the middle, so it looks neater.

WARNING: As with the constrictor knot, never tie the strangle knot around any part of the body.

Step 1

Loop the working end over the rail or bundle to which it is being tied, and lead it toward the right, as shown.

Step 2

Repeat Step 1, taking the working end over the rail to the right of the previous wrap. Make sure the working end emerges in the middle, i.e., with the loop to the left, and the hanging part to the right.

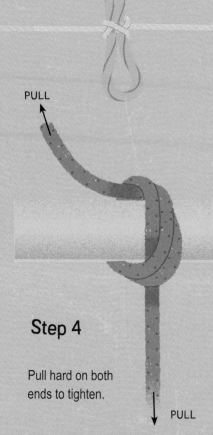

PULL

Step 3

Lead the working end to the right, then thread it up and under the wrapped cord, to the left.

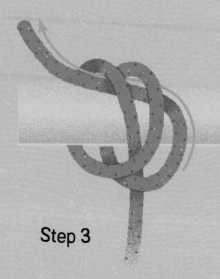

Step 4

Pull hard on both ends to tighten.

PULL

Uses

Use a thin cord to tie a strangle Knot around a fraying rope.

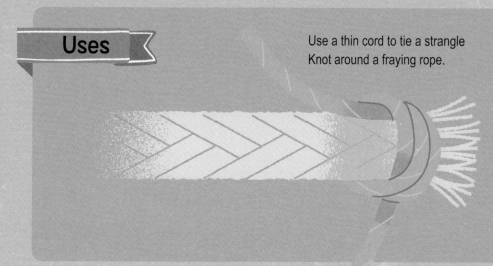

Reef Knot

The reef knot is a binding knot and can be remembered as "left over right and under, right over left and under." It lies flat once tied and works well binding a roll of cloth. To undo, give a sharp tug on one end. The reef knot shouldn't be used to join ropes where the material or size of the ropes is different as it may come undone.

WORKING END   WORKING END

Step 1

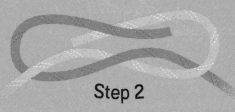

Position the two cords like this, with the two working ends loosely wrapping around each other.

Uses

An emergency first-aid sling or a bandage is finished with a reef knot.

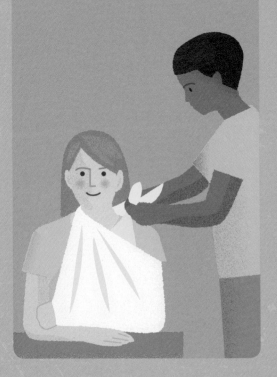

Step 2

Now take the working end on the left and lay it over the other working end, as shown.

PULL   PULL

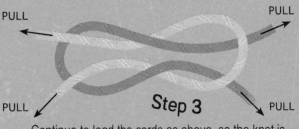

PULL   ## Step 3   PULL

Continue to lead the cords as above, so the knot is neat and symmetrical. Pull all ends to tighten.

Glossary

Back-up knot An extra knot added for security, especially where failure would be especially dangerous.

Bend A knot for joining two (or more) ropes.

Bight A curve in a rope. If the curve is completely closed it becomes a loop.

Cord Technically, material less than 10 mm (0.4 inches) in diameter. See also **Rope.**

Eye A small loop in a rope end.

Half hitch A simple knot made by passing the end of a rope around itself, another rope or an object and then through its own loop. The same structure as an overhand knot.

Hanging part The end of a rope that isn't used to create a knot, when the rope is suspended from another object. See also **Standing part.**

Hitch A knot for attaching a rope to an object (e.g. a ring) or another rope where the two ropes are not being tied together to form one.

Knot security A knot's resistance to slipping.

Knot strength The strength of the rope once it has been knotted—a knot reduces the original strength of rope.

Lead The direction the working end of a rope takes.

Loop A circle in a rope, the ends of which are either joined or cross over one another.

Noose A loop that is not of fixed size, i.e. it can easily be adjusted. See also **Slip knot.**

Rope Technically, to be called rope, material must be at least 10 mm (0.4 inches) in diameter, however the term is used loosely to describe any thick cordage from about 6 mm (0.2 inches).

Round turn A complete turn of rope when wrapped around an object (or another rope).

Shackle Horseshoe-shaped metal fitting attached to a chain or fitting such as an eye bolt. It has a removable pin to close it.

Sling A circle of rope or tape either knotted at the ends or stitched (in the case of tape).

Slip Knot A knot tied in the end of a rope using an overhand knot around the standing part. See also **Noose.**

Slipped knot Knot where the end of the rope has been tucked to enable the knot to be undone by pulling on the end.

Standing part The end of a rope that isn't used to create a knot. See also **Hanging part.**

Stopper knot A knot to create a thicker point in a rope, used to stop a rope from slipping through a hole.

Thimble A metal or plastic fitting inserted into the eye of a rope. Usually heart-shaped, but sometimes circular, it has a groove into which the rope fits. Helps to stop wear on the rope.

Tie-in knot Knot used to attach a rope to a climber's harness.

Working end The end of a rope used to create a knot.

Index